This book belongs to

_____

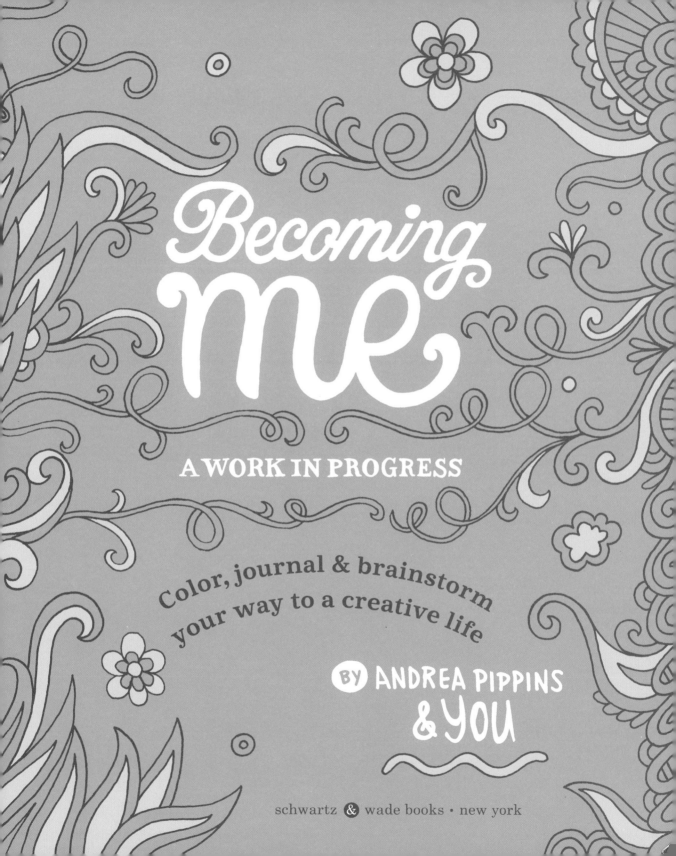

Becoming Me

A WORK IN PROGRESS

Color, journal & brainstorm your way to a creative life

BY ANDREA PIPPINS & YOU

schwartz & wade books · new york

For Isabel Nunes Martins and all the young women
in the world pursuing their creative dreams

Copyright © 2016 by Andrea Pippins
Author photo courtesy of Danielle Finney

All rights reserved. Published in the United States by Schwartz & Wade Books, an imprint of
Random House Children's Books, a division of Penguin Random House LLC, New York.

Schwartz & Wade Books and the colophon are trademarks of Penguin Random House LLC.

Visit us on the Web! randomhousekids.com

Educators and librarians, for a variety of teaching tools,
visit us at RHTeachersLibrarians.com

The text of this book is set in Din.

The illustrations were rendered in Micron and Uniball pens,
Sharpie markers, and watercolor.

ISBN 978-0-399-55915-0

MANUFACTURED IN CHINA
2 4 6 8 10 9 7 5 3 1
First Edition

"You can't use up creativity.
The more you use, the more you have."
—Maya Angelou

Because of my experience as an artist, a graphic designer, and an educator, I am frequently asked for advice about living a creative life. I truly enjoy sharing what I have learned with others, but at the same time, I am well aware that because we are all unique and have different life experiences, it's important for everyone to find their own creative way. What I'm sharing with you in the following pages are techniques and practices that have helped and continue to help me be creative every day. I believe living a creative life is best achieved by being curious, passionate, and inspired; so pick up a pen, pencil, paintbrush, or marker and start expressing yourself.

How can you nurture your creativity every day?
Can you draw or paint for 15 minutes? Look at some
art? Write poetry? Write some ideas below.

CREATE A COLOR PALETTE

1. Choose a base color. This can be any color you like. I like this green.

2. Choose a ground color that is darker than the first. A darker green goes well with my first color.

3. Choose a highlight color. Use this as an accent. This light seafoam blue fits nicely.

4. Once you figure out your first three colors, you can add others that feel like they are a part of your color family. Yellow adds a nice pop to my palette.

YOU TRY

Color the circles with your color palette.

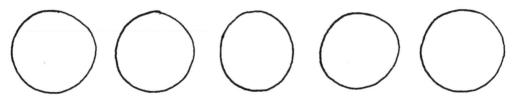

COLOR

THESE DOODLES
using your
new palette

1. look at letters & words

The best way to understand how to make letters is to examine them. Browse through books and look online and in magazines, paying attention to the different kinds of letter forms. Look closely at the way letters connect in script and at the differences between capital and lowercase letters. Record what you see here.

@. experiment with tools

Different kinds of tools will give your letter forms
a different look. Try hand-lettering with pens, markers,
paintbrushes, and pencils. See what you like and determine
which tool will work best in different situations. For example,
I like to use Micron pens for detailed lettering, but for me,
watercolor is best for flowy type. Practice in the space below.

③. practice & play

The only way to make your hand-lettering skills stronger is to practice. Experiment and play with different styles! Use the space below to have fun with letters.

be sure to fill the page

Doodle and hand-letter the
conversations you had today.

KINDS OF LETTERING

fun
serif

fun
sans serif

FUN
thin

FUN
chunky

decorative

script

bubble

FUN

3-D

Hand-Letter Your Name

Doodle your name using the lettering styles from the previous page.

serif

sans serif

thin

chunky

decorative

script

bubble

3-D

ORK

OF

BEAUTY

can G

COM

PHOTOGRAPHER: P SHOT ON LOCATIO

es, summer = girl,

the Mexico,

Mexico,

Thursday, January 20th from 11:30am to 8:30pm

Collect: Type

To practice your lettering, collect existing letters to refer to. I like to clip pages from magazines and old books to add cool typography to my image library. Add your own found letters to this page. Layer them to add to the collage.

Power gir

NEW FACES of FE ISM

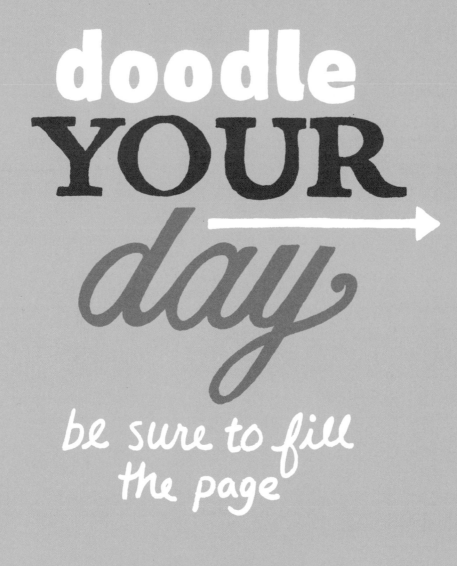

doodle **YOUR** *day*

be sure to fill the page

What did you do today? Doodle the activities here.

Tips on Analyzing Art

Looking at art is wonderful, but it's even more amazing when you understand how to analyze what you see. Here are a few tips on how to examine art you might see online, at a museum, or out and about.

Context

When looking at art, it's helpful to understand the circumstances surrounding the work. Find out the time period when the artwork was created. What political or cultural events were happening? Did something of note occur in the artist's life? These are things that might have influenced the work you are seeing.

Subject

What is the main image? A person, an object, or a place? Consider the importance of the subject and its relationship to the artist. What meaning does it give to the overall work?

I ♥ Art

Medium

What materials are being used in the artwork? Paint, ink, wood? Does the medium give the work a special meaning? Why do you think the artist used this medium for this piece?

Composition

As you are admiring art, pay attention to the placement of the subject and any other elements. Where does your eye go first? Next? Last? Do you think there is an order of visual importance?

color

Color can tell us a lot about a piece of work. It can tell us about the mood or message. When looking at the colors, think about whether they are meant to evoke a certain feeling or have a symbolic meaning. Like red, white, and blue for the U.S. flag or bright colors for fun.

emotion

When you see a piece of art, be aware of how it makes you feel. Pay attention to the emotions it evokes. Does it make you sad, anxious, angry, excited? Consider whether this was the intention of the artist.

foreground/ background

Examine how the artwork is organized. What is in the foreground and what is in the background? Why do you think the artist placed the images this way?

TEXTURE

When looking at artwork, try to get as close as you can. Look at the brushstrokes in a painting. The layering of papers in a collage. The material used in a sculpture. Consider what the texture adds to the image. Think about the work and energy that went into creating that texture.

SCALE

The size of a piece of art can tell us a lot. If you're seeing it in person, how does the size allow you to interact with the piece? Do you have to get really close to see the details? Or is it so big that it feels like it's taking over the space?

Malick Sidibé · photography CORITA KENT

HENRI MATISSE

I ♥ KENT

NY · MILTON GLASER

mixed media

Jean-Michel Basquiat

CRAFT · Alexander Girard · Yayoi

Kehinde Wiley Candy Chang KUSAMA

♥ painting

INSTALLATION

MICKALENE THOMAS

What Do ⬭YOU⬭ SEE?

Now let's look at some art from my list of favorite artists and designers, or choose one that you're curious about. Go to the library or a museum, or search online for information about that artist and his or her work. Choose one piece and answer the following questions.

 1. What's the artist's name? Write down the name of the piece you selected to analyze. Include when it was created.

_____

_____

 2. What medium did the artist use? Describe the textures, color, and subject.

_____

_____

 3. What do you think the artist was trying to say with this piece? What does it mean to you?

_____

_____

 4. How does the piece make you feel?

_____

_____

DRAW WHAT you see:

Use the space below to visually capture what you see in the piece you chose. You can draw exactly what you see or sections of the piece. This exercise will allow you to practice a different way of creating imagery.

BE INSPIRED BY

POP
art

I love being inspired by various art movements. It's cool to see what other artists have done before me. Let's be inspired by the pop art movement. Look online or go to the library and find images of art by Andy Warhol or Roy Lichtenstein. Design a postcard of your hometown in the pop art style.

COLLAGE LIKE
MICKALENE THOMAS

Mickalene Thomas is an amazing collage artist. When you research her, you will see that she uses rhinestones, acrylic paint, and patterned paper to produce her images. Collage an image of a friend using similar materials.

Here's what you'll need:

Paper, glue, scissors, rhinestones, acrylic paint, paintbrushes, and found paper (preferably patterned).

Here's what to do:

Take a picture of your subject to use as a guide, or use your imagination. Then plan out your page. Mickalene always has her subject surrounded by patterns. Be inspired by this and think about what you should make sparkle with your rhinestones.

CUT PAPER LIKE

HENRI MATISSE

In his later years, after developing some physical challenges that made painting difficult, Henri Matisse began creating images with cut paper. Be inspired by his technique. Look for images of his paper cutouts. Pay attention to his use of color and how he abstracted figures, plants, and animals. Try your own paper cutouts. Create an image of a plant in your home (or outside) using the cut-paper method.

Here's what you'll need:

A large sheet of paper (if you want something bigger than the next page), colored sheets of construction paper, scissors, and glue

Here's what to do:

Once you find a plant to be your muse, choose a color you will use for your cut-paper plant. Use scissors to cut out the shape of your plant from the paper. Pay attention to the individual leaves and the plant as a whole. Is the plant potted? If so, use another color for the pot.

BE INSPIRED BY

STREET
ART

Using the work of Basquiat, Swoon, or Shepard Fairey as inspiration, create a street image of your favorite animal. Research the work of these artists and think about how you would create your own street art style.

MAKE DOTS LIKE
Yayoi KUSAMA

Yayoi Kusama is known for her patterns using dots. Explore her style and notice her use of various colors, sizes, and placements in her dot patterns. Using dots as a motif, design your own clothing (shoes, T-shirt, dress, pants, etc.) or accessory (tote bag, purse, hat, etc.) item.

Here's what you'll need:

For this exercise you can draw or paint the dots, or use the cut-paper technique. Grab the materials you need based on the medium you select: watercolor, acrylic paint, markers, pens, construction paper, found paper, or colored pencils.

Here's what to do:

First draw a silhouette of the clothing or accessory item of your choice. If you want a base color for your item, fill in the silhouette with color. Now add your dots. Play with the scale of your dots. They can be the same size or completely different.

use color like CORITA KENT

Corita Kent captured her audience's attention with her dynamic use of color. Bright or contrasting colors added visual interest to her messages of social activism.
Be inspired by her use of color and create a positive message in bold letter forms using a vibrant palette.

Here's what you'll need:

Paint, markers, or colored pencils.
You can also try cutting letters for your words out of paper.

Here's what to do:

First determine what your inspiring message will be. Plan your layout on the page and hand-letter the message. Make sure the letters are big and bold. Fill in the lettering with vibrant colors.
If you're using paper, make sure to cut from bright colors.

DESIGN LIKE
MILTON GLASER

Milton Glaser is an illustrator and graphic designer best known for his I ♥ NY logo created in 1976. Here's your chance to design your own I ♥ logo. Look at the original I ♥ NY logo and then look at other iterations of the same idea. Think about at least four people you love. Use their names, nicknames, or initials to make an I ♥ logo for each person.

Here's what you'll need:

For this exercise you can use any drawing tool you'd like.

Here's what to do:

After you have selected the people you'll design a logo for, start sketching the layout of each. Determine whether it will be stacked or all on one line. Consider what kind of lettering you'll use. Try a different kind to match the personality of each person.

DOODLE YOUR FAVORITE OUTFIT

Practice your doodling style by doodling things around you. I like to doodle some of my favorite things, like items in my wardrobe. Label your doodles to practice your hand-lettering.

HERE'S MINE

bangles

army-green tunic tied in the front

Booties

leather skirt

stud earrings

Black leggings

YOUR TURN

Quiet moment

Take a moment to think about and write down things that
make you smile. A family member? A favorite dish?
A good book? List some below.

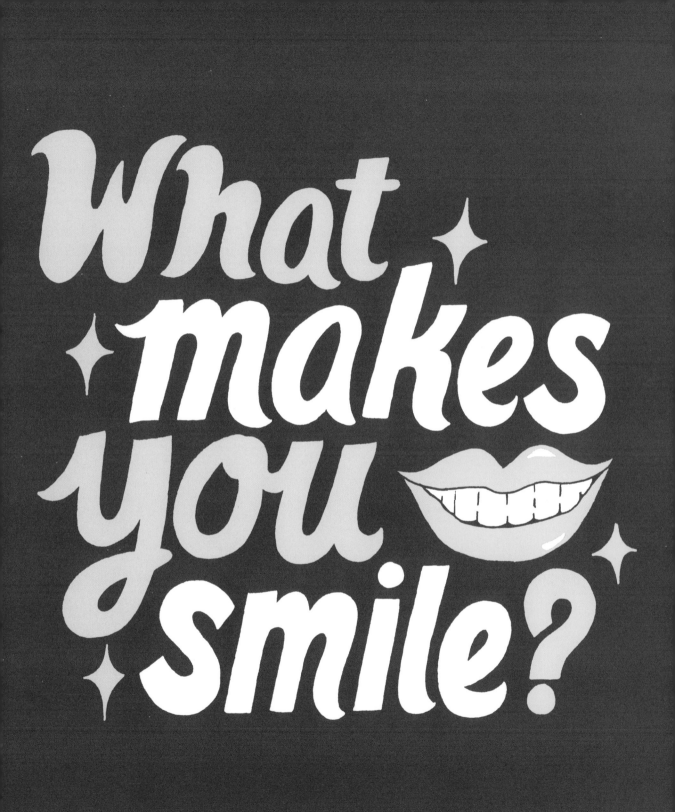

COLOR THE PAISLEYS

SPEAK YOUR MIND!

Is there a cause you strongly believe in? Something you want the world to know about? T-shirts and buttons are great ways to share your beliefs. Use this space to design your own T-shirt and buttons.

Fill in these buttons with designs that speak your mind.

doodle
YOUR
DAY

be sure to fill the page

Doodle something that made you happy today.

Quiet moment:

Have you ever been afraid to speak up? What happened?
Why didn't you speak up? How did you feel?
Would you handle the situation differently now?

_____

_____

_____

_____

_____

_____

_____

_____

_____

_____

_____

_____

How to Mind-Map

Mind-mapping is a great way to brainstorm words, images, and ideas. When I do an illustration, I create a mind-map to help me think of words related to the main topic. That way I see beyond the obvious ideas. Here's my mind-map for the word **jungle**. I used some of the words in my mind-map to create the doodle you see on the facing page.

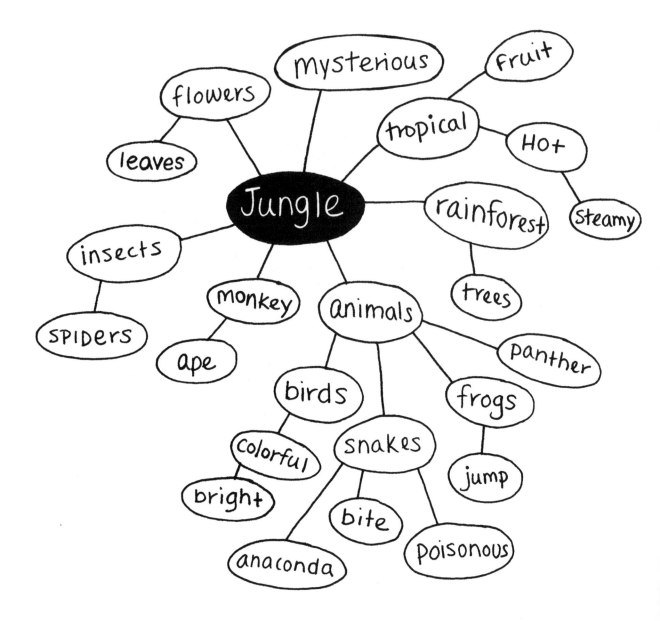

Your Mind-Map

Now it's your turn to make a mind-map. Use the word ocean. Write the word in the circle in the center of the page. Then make a web of more circles, filling them with words that come to mind from the word ocean. After you've exhausted your ideas, try extending circles from your new words.

Use words from your mind-map to doodle all things
ocean-related. Don't forget to fill the page!

Ever feel scared to follow your dreams?
In the space below, write down why, and then brainstorm
things you can do to make sure you follow your dreams.

BIG DREAMS are not the dreams we've seen others accomplish or the ones we already know we can achieve. Big, powerful dreams are the dreams that blow our minds when we say them out loud, the ones that give us goose bumps when we write them down, or the ones we have no idea how to make happen—we just believe we will.

Capture your big dreams in the dream bubbles on the next page.

CREATE A COLOR PALETTE

1. Find an image with colors you like. Look at photographs or in a magazine. Cut out the image.

2. Examine the image. What colors stand out or are used most? In this photo I took in Rio de Janeiro, I was drawn to the pinks and purples. Then I noticed that there is a lot of bluish gray with pops of light blue. Those became my four main colors.

YOUR TURN

DOODLE CHALLENGE

OUTER SPACE

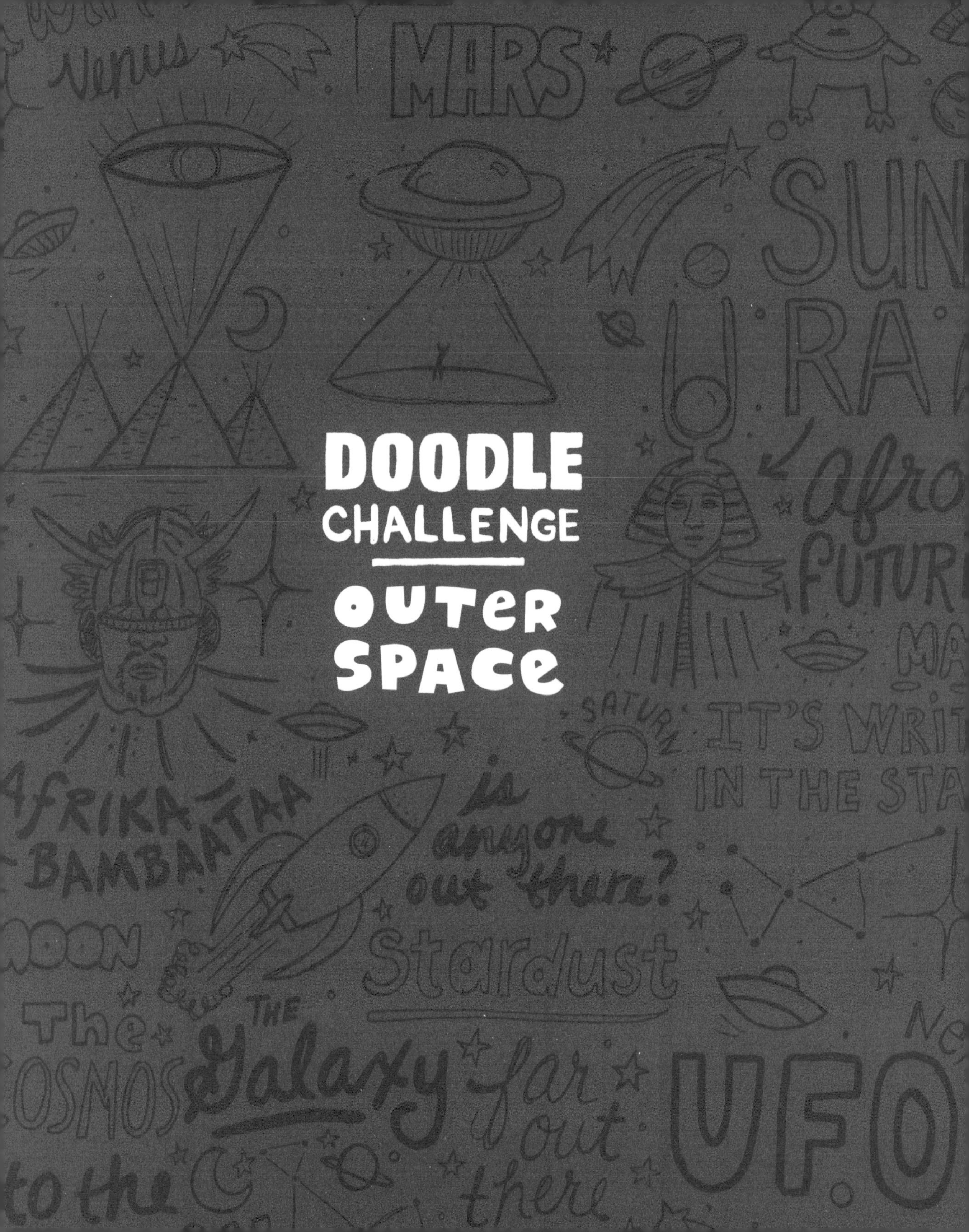

Fill the page with doodles of all things outer space.
Think of images like stars, planets, comets,
astronauts, etc. Use the Internet if you need a
reference for what something looks like.

Collect: Found Paper

I love collecting scraps of paper. They are perfect for collages
and digital illustrations and for inspiring hand-lettering.
I've been collecting numbers from ticket stubs for years.
Find your own and store them in folders or in a box.
Try gluing or taping some of them to this page.

1183417

0798

day 6pm.

Super Plan Associate
754 B St. Nicholas Ave.
Corner of 148th Street
New York, NY 10032
212-234-8760

V.P.

DATE 06 X 29 05 $ ¢

18-073

3

5

6

00713

3568

CLAIM CHECK
PLEASE PRESENT THIS STUB
TO CASHIER WHEN CALLING
FOR YOUR VEHICLE.
Thank You.

1180

TICKET
509668
MMF INDUSTRIES

240
CLAIM CHECK
IN CASE OF ANY LOSS,
CLAIM BEFORE LEAVING
Not Responsible for
Contents of Garments or
anything left overnight

6398

1943

TICKET
597386
MMF INDUSTRIES

0778

1180

56831
DRIVERS RECEIPT
PRESENT WHEN CAR IS DELIVERED

79684

_____ MAKE
_____ MODEL

3568

Swirls & Curls

Also known as flourishes, swirls and curls are great ways to add embellishments to your hand-lettering or illustrations. I use them all the time (you can find some throughout this book). Here's a little guide on how to make your own.

like an "S" on its side

add loops

add curls

add leaves and flowers

YOUR TURN

try a curl

loops

add leaves

add flowers

long curl

add leaves

YOU TRY

FINISH THE FLOWERS

Using the flowers on the facing page as your guide,
add your own petals, leaves, and flourishes to the flowers below.

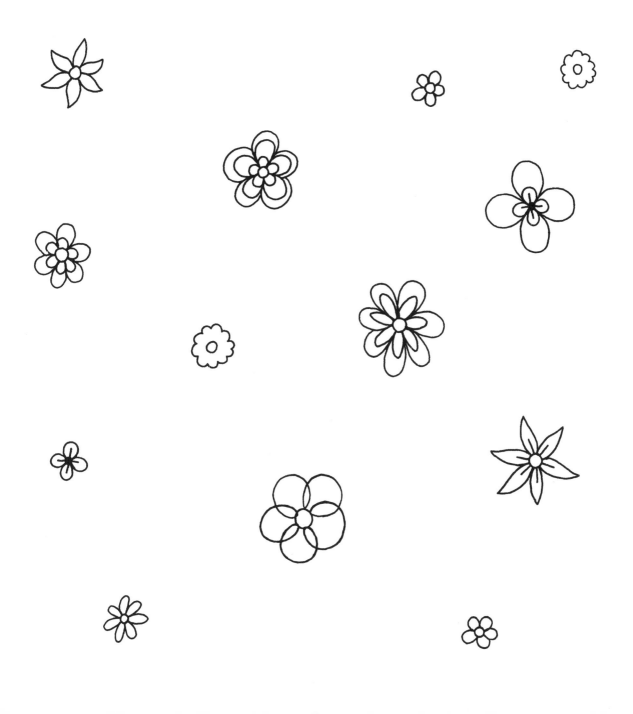

DOODLE

YOUR

DAY

be sure to fill the page

What was the weather like today? Doodle the weather and what you wore.

I used my imagination to make the grass whatever color I wanted it to be.

—Whoopi Goldberg

BE CURIOUS AND

SEE THE WORLD.

Quiet moment:

Traveling is a great way to learn about different people, cultures, and climates. Are there places you'd like to visit? List five of them below. Look up those places online and doodle images related to each.

1. _____

2. _____

3. _____

4. _____

5. _____

Food & Travel DOODLES

I love to travel and I love to eat. During a trip to New Orleans, I doodled some of my favorite meals. This became a fun reminder of the delicious eats I had there. Use the space below to capture your most memorable meals from your favorite trip.

PROMOÇÃO
CALDO de CANA
PASTEL
COXINHA * KIBE
EMPADA
BOLINHO de AIPIM
GUARAVITA

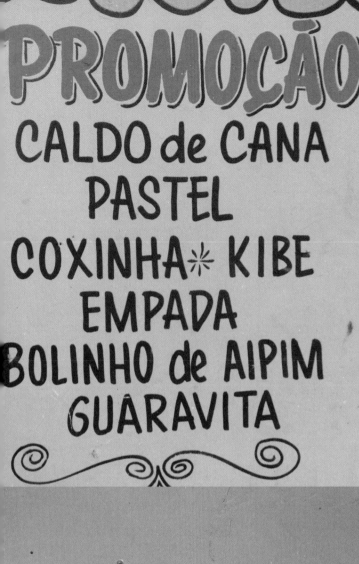

PADARIA

O. R

Ate

rmamos

v. Major A

DRAW Letters

When I travel, I always photograph hand-lettering I see on signs and walls. Then I try to draw what I see in those photographs. The next time you travel, take your own photos and practice your lettering by drawing what you see.

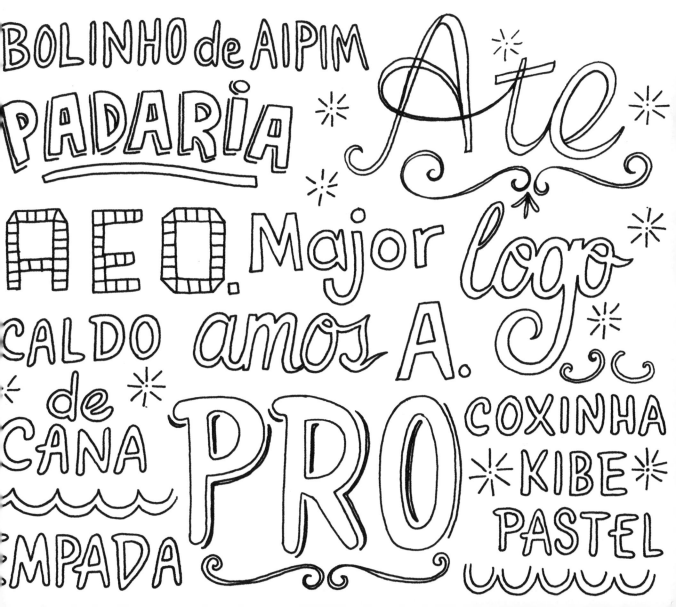

BOLINHO de AIPIM

PADARIA

Até

A E O.

Major

logo

CALDO

amos A.

de CANA

PRO

COXINHA

KIBE

PASTEL

MPADA

Who do you love? What do you love?
How do you love? Fill the page with doodles
of people, places, feelings, activities,
and ways you love.

DRAWING LINE (with) emotion

Give your drawings emotion by making the line reflect the feelings you are trying to convey. Using the examples below as a guide, try drawing your own lines that are happy or angry, nervous or bold.

angry/aggressive

happy/free

nervous/unsure

bold/loud

YOUR TURN

Be BOLD,
BRIGHT &
Beautiful
as you are

What makes you bold, bright, and beautiful? Write your answers below in phrases, a story, a poem, or an essay.

_____

_____

_____

_____

_____

_____

_____

_____

_____

_____

_____

_____

_____

_____

_____

_____

_____

_____

590B-7 ^D
Award Blue †

Tile Blue

collect: Patterns

I'm always collecting patterns for inspiration and
for collage. Whenever I see them in a magazine or
old book, I make sure to cut some out for my collection.
Go through old magazines or books and look for patterns.
Cut them out and glue or tape them to this page.

FINISH THESE TEXTILES

I love collecting textiles. Their colors and patterns inspire me.
I also enjoy drawing them. In the quilt and rug on these pages,
add your own pattern designs; then add color.

Doodle your personal story.
Consider creating a map of what you've
done up to this point. Include where you have
lived, schooling, passions, and hobbies.

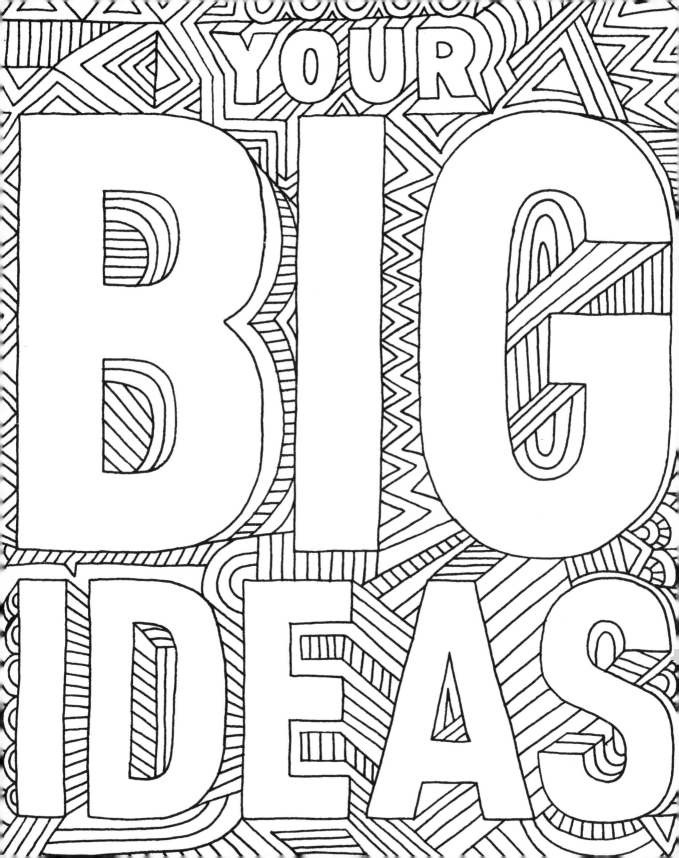

WRITE THEM DOWN HERE↓

collect: Texture

Found texture is great for creating artwork. My favorite textures to collect are found on the insides of security envelopes (see left). The envelopes that our bills and junk mail come in have really cool patterns that I like to use in my illustrations. Look for texture in unexpected places. Look at your junk mail and see if you can find some fun textures. Cut them out and glue or tape them to this page.

Quiet moment

Take some time to write down thoughts about who you are. What do you like? What makes you upset? What are you passionate about? List some of your personal characteristics below.

_____

_____

_____

_____

_____

_____

_____

_____

_____

_____

_____

_____

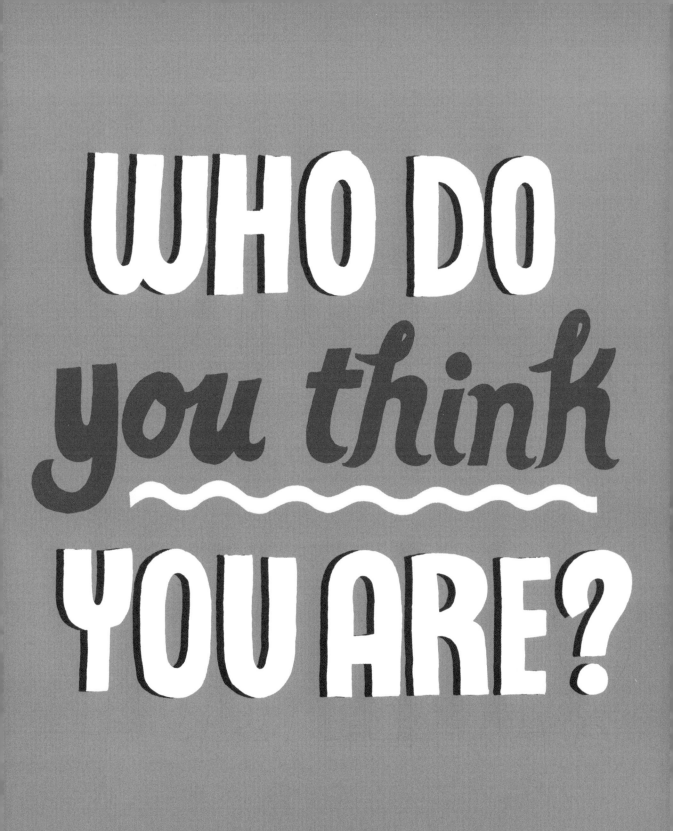

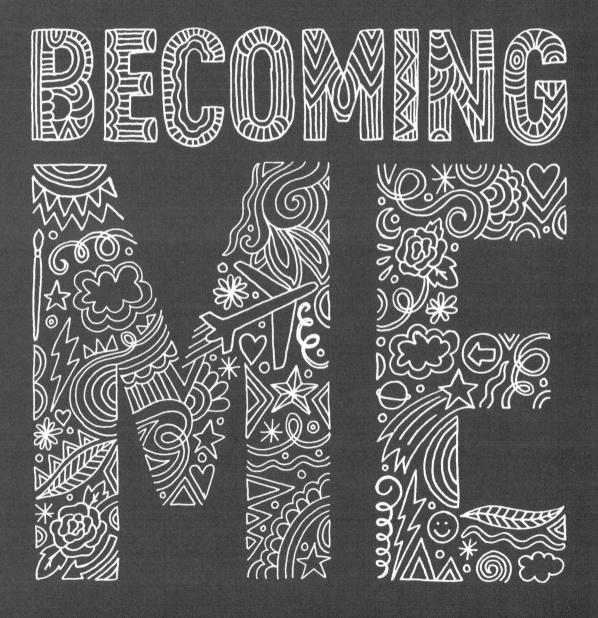

Fill in this "BECOMING ME" with your own style of doodles.

Selfie Portrait

1. Using your phone or a camera, take a selfie. Make sure the lighting is good so you can see the details. Try using natural light by taking the photo outside or next to a window.

2. Choose the materials you'd like to use. Will your selfie portrait be in watercolor, paint, pen, or marker? Will it be a collage? It's up to you. Choose a medium that reflects your mood or personality.

3. Try doing a few rough pencil sketches on a separate sheet of paper. When you have a general idea of how you think your portrait should look, go ahead and start drawing, painting, or collaging it into the frame.

4. When you're finished with your portrait, color the frame. Then share your masterpiece! I would love to see what you created. Use the #BecomingME hashtag so I can find you.

What's on your mind?

What did you think about today? Capture your thoughts in these thought bubbles. They can be in the form of hand-lettering or doodles.

watercolor flower doodles

Finish these flowers by adding your own doodled
leaves, petals, and flourishes.

fun (WITH) Collage

Here are some quick tips for having fun with collage.

look for interesting images

Look through magazines, old books, junk mail, and catalogs for images with texture, figures, and colors.

play with scale

Your collage doesn't have to be literal. Match a tiny building with a huge flower or put an insect atop a small car. Challenge how we usually see things in the world.

make unexpected images work together

Because the collage can be anything you can imagine, create a world that brings together unexpected things. Make flowers grow in snow or people stand on water.

plan before you glue

Once you know what the image will be, start laying out your papers. Try different compositions before gluing down the images.

add doodles or painted color

Add details to your collages by incorporating doodles and painted elements. This will give your collages more depth.

Here's what you'll need:

scissors

magazines

Glue

TAPE

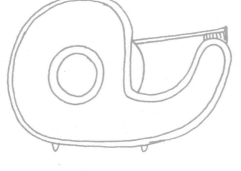

NEWS

PHOTOS

newspaper

Collage:  a face

 Decide what kind of face you will collage. Someone you know? Your own face? Or an imaginary person?

 Once you've determined what face you will collage, begin collecting images. You can be literal and look for eyes, nose, and a mouth or find images that can suggest those elements based on your placement of them.

 Play with the placement of your face collage. Don't forget to think about scale and composition.

 Now you're ready to glue. Once your collage is dry, add doodles or painted color if you choose.

Collage: a landscape

 1. Decide what kind of landscape you will collage. A place you visited? An imaginary town?

 2. Once you've determined what place you will collage, start collecting images for the landscape. You can be literal and look for mountains or landmasses, or find images that can suggest those elements based on your placement of them. You can also use texture to suggest different parts of the landscape, like grainy paper for sand or a green pattern for a forest.

 3. Play with the placement of your landscape collage. Don't forget to think about scale and composition.

 4. Now you're ready to glue. Once your collage is dry, add doodles or painted color if you choose.

GETTING READY
DOODLES

Doodle the items you use every day.

hand-letter
YOUR
FRIENDS'
names
be sure to fill the page
→

Create a Mood-board

Here's what you'll need

GLUE

SCISSORS

PAPER or POSTER BOARD

BOOKS and MAGAZINES

TAPE

PEN

Mood-boards are a great way to capture an idea or project. I often like to create mood-boards to display all in one place images, colors, and patterns that inspire me. In the space below, or on a sheet of poster board, glue images that inspire you. Try doing a theme, like plant life or galaxies. When you're done, hang the board somewhere you can see it daily. It may spark an idea for your next creation.

Quiet moment

Below, write about someone you admire.
Why do you admire them? What questions
would you like to ask this person?

_____

_____

_____

_____

_____

_____

_____

_____

_____

_____

_____

_____

_____

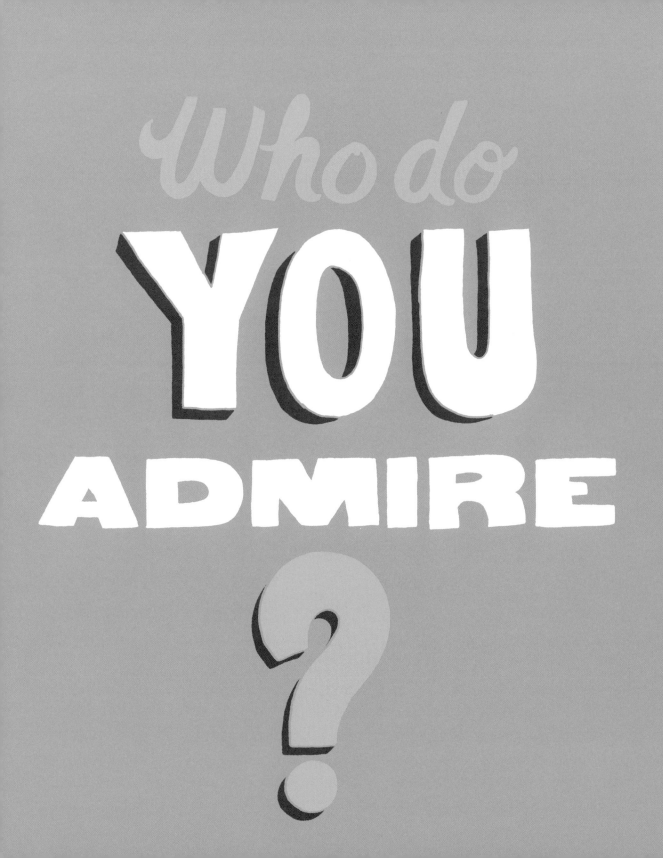

Your Creative Goal Map

Do you have a creative goal? Like designing wedding invitations for a friend? Making a gift? Learning how to paint with acrylics? Use this map to reach your goal. Write that goal in the top right bubble. Brainstorm ways to get there, and plug them into the other bubbles based on the order you think makes sense. Start with where you are today (bottom left bubble).

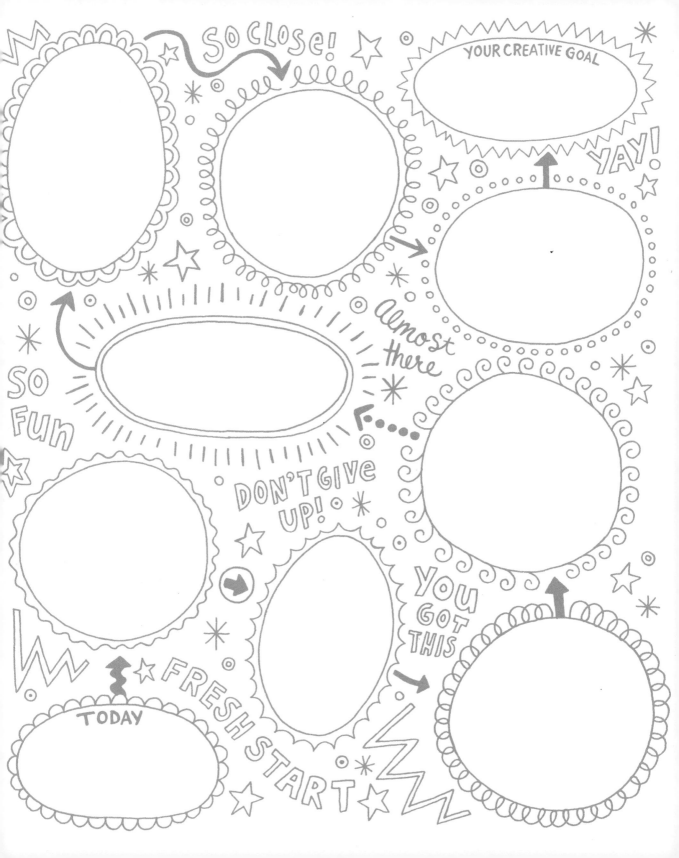

SO CLOSE!

YOUR CREATIVE GOAL

YAY!

Almost there

SO FUN

DON'T GIVE UP!

YOU GOT THIS

FRESH START

TODAY

I love listening to music when I'm creating. Artists like
Erykah Badu, Lianne La Havas, Quadron, and A Tribe Called
Quest are always on repeat in my studio. Do you have
a go-to playlist that gets you in a creative groove?
List the songs here (try hand-lettering them). When you're
done, add a design to the cassette tape on the facing page.

(1.) _____

(2.) _____

(3.) _____

(4.) _____

(5.) _____

(6.) _____

(7.) _____

(8.) _____

(9.) _____

(10.) _____

Where did you go today? Doodle a map of your travels.

WAYS TO BE INSPIRED

Need a little inspiration? Here are some suggestions
for ways to see the world differently.

Be CURIOUS

TAKE A WALK

look at art

visit a museum

read poetry

DAYDREAM

write a story

try something new

RELAX

visit a new place

TAKE A CREATIVE RISK

READ ABOUT INSPIRING PEOPLE

PLAY OUTSIDE

GO TO A LIBRARY

BUY flowers

laugh

embrace nature

LOOK AT COLOR

listen to music

Visit a flea market

Look out your window or go for a walk.
Doodle what you see: trees, birds,
houses, cars, signs, buses—anything
in your neighborhood.

Doodle on Random Things

Sometimes I like to doodle on random things like magazine subscription cards. What about you? Have you ever doodled on an old T-shirt, sneakers, or a paper cup? Use a marker and give it a try.

finish this pattern

Add your own little doodles, decorative elements,
and triangles to finish this chevron pattern.

TIPS FOR SHARING YOUR ART ONLINE

Putting your art out into the world is courageous and fun. It gives you the opportunity to get feedback and connect with others who may have similar interests.

1. Choose online platforms that work for you. Maybe a blog is the way to go, or maybe something more instant like Instagram is more your style. Or try multiple platforms at once. It's up to you!

2. Quality matters. Take good photos. Use natural light for photographs, and share images that people can see clearly. Make sure what you share shines!

3. Be yourself. Your style and creations are unique to you. Always stay true to yourself and your art, whether it's online or in person.

Customize these images with doodles and color. Then share
your masterpieces with your friends on social media.

Make this message reflect
your creativity.

Color this with your favorite
color palette.

Make this circle into something special.

Share a thought from your day.

Watercolor Faces

Make these watercolor dots into faces by doodling
features, hair, and other details.

finish this pattern

Add your own doodles and details to make these motifs
more intricate. When you're done, add color!

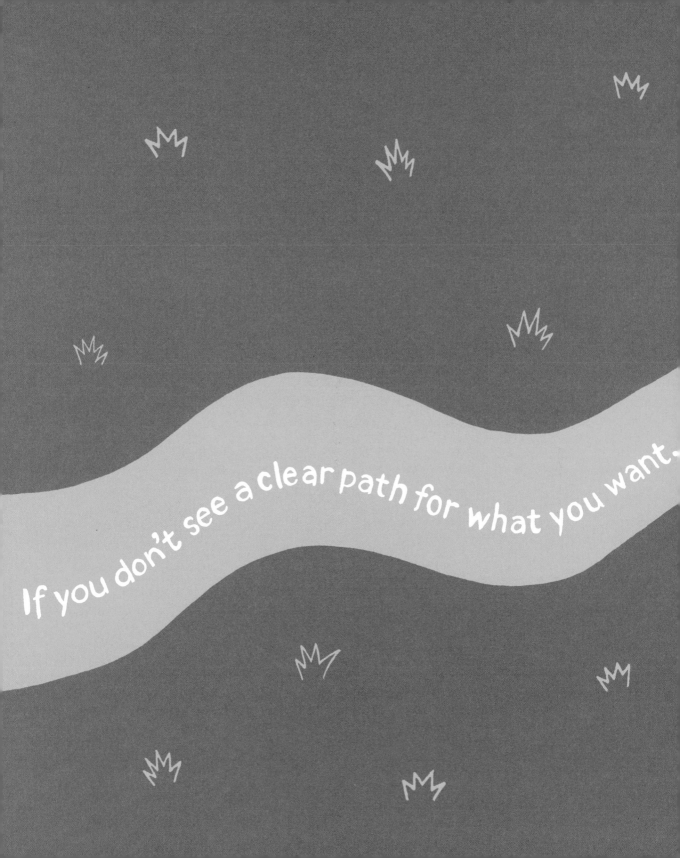

If you don't see a clear path for what you want,

sometimes you have to make it yourself.

– Mindy Kaling

I feel CREATIVE when...

When do you feel most creative? What kinds of projects
make you feel at your creative best? List them here.

sketches

Notes

NOTES

sketches

SKETCHES

notes

thank
YOU

To my parents, Samir Bhur,
Rachael Cole, Lee Wade, and all
who have supported my dreams.
Thank you all for supporting me
during this creative adventure.